MW01244680

My Favorite Fan

Mending Bones, Making Friends

by Timothy LeeBurton, M.D.
with Christy Steele

LeeBurton Educational Publishing
1112 South Holly Drive
Sioux Falls, SD 57105

Web Site Address: www.leeburtonpublishing.com

Library of Congress Control Number: 2005925483

ISBN 0976830701

Credits
Designer: Jennifer Pfeiffer
Editor: Christy Steele
Illustrations: Jason Walton

Content has been reviewed by: Timothy LeeBurton, M.D., Orthopedic Surgeon

Printed in the USA

05 06 07 08 09 10 CG 10 9 8 7 6 5 4 3 2 1

My Favorite Fan

is the story of two boys who become friends after an accident that happens while one of the boys is playing baseball. Their differences disappear as they learn valuable lessons about life.

Features

How Bones Work 9
Why Bones Break 10
Different Kinds of Fractures 10
First Aid for Bones 10
How an X-ray Machine Works 15
All About Casts 17
When a Bone Breaks 23

My Photo 26
Signatures 26
Tell Your Story: "When My Arm Broke" . . . 27
X-ray Diagram 28
Internet Sites 29
Books To Read 29
Glossary 30
Index 32

I held my bat high and waited. "Eyes on the ball," I told myself. Just when I was ready to hit, Devin put his fingers through the wire fence behind home plate and screamed, "We want a pitcher, not a belly itcher!"

I turned to frown and shake my head at him and ended up swinging just one second too late. My bat swished through empty air. "Strike two," the umpire shouted.

It wasn't fair. I blamed my strike on Devin Smith, the loudmouth fan. He'd been at team tryouts, but he couldn't hit, couldn't pitch, and couldn't catch, so he didn't make the team. Ever since, Devin had shown up at all our games, sitting in the front row with his dad and leading the rest of the fans in screaming and stomping contests. For each game he wore a T-shirt with "Rockbirds" painted on it, and his baseball cap was always turned sideways. The coach said we should be nice to Devin because he had so much team spirit. But I thought Devin made things worse most of the time. Some teams had good-luck charms, but the Rockbirds were stuck with bad-luck Devin. I wanted Devin to go home. Maybe then I could get a hit again.

My teammate Jamie stood on third base. "You can do it, Adam," he yelled. "Bring me home."

I had two strikes against me, so this was my last chance. The pitcher whipped the baseball toward me. I watched the round, white ball come closer and swung hard when it was almost in front of me. Finally, my bat whacked the ball, and it sailed deep into the outfield. It felt great to hit the ball hard.

I ran safely to first, but the ball was still going. So I kept moving, too. I rounded second base and sped toward third. I paused at third for a second to catch my breath. All the fans were on their feet cheering. Devin stood behind the fence and jumped up and down. "Run home!" he screamed. "Home! Home! Home!"

As I started running again, an outfielder threw the ball to the catcher at home plate. "No way you're going to get me out," I thought. I ran as fast as I could. Just as the catcher was about to catch the ball, I saw home plate just a couple steps away.

There was only one thing I could do to stop the catcher from tagging me out. "Eat my dust," I said and dove headfirst toward home, stretching my arm as far as it could go until my fingers touched the edge of the base. The umpire spread his arms out from his sides. "Safe!" he yelled.

But I really wasn't safe. My body was moving too fast to stop. All my weight pressed on my

arm, jamming it into the plate. My arm bent weirdly, and something snapped deep inside it. Pain throbbed outward from below my elbow. I tried to lift my arm, but it wouldn't move. It was like it didn't take orders from my brain anymore. I didn't even try to stand up. I just bit my lower lip to keep from crying.

My coach knelt down and looked at me holding my arm. "Is it broken?" he asked.

"I don't know. It hurts."

How Bones Work

Bones make up the skeleton, a hard framework that supports and protects the soft organs and tissue in our bodies. Support from our skeleton makes it possible for us to stand and sit. Without bones, we would be just a pile of skin.

The bones in your body are alive. Bones grow as you grow. You have 206 adult bones. Bones stop growing when you reach about 25 years old.

Minerals, cells, and proteins are part of every bone. And every bone has several different layers. Each layer has its own job to do. The thin, outer layer is the periosteum. It brings food to the bone. Hard, compact bone makes the next layer. The inner layer contains jelly-like bone marrow. Bone marrow makes blood cells for our body.

FYI

Why Bones Break

Our bones are strong. After all, they hold up our whole body. Even so, bones sometimes fracture, or break, if we put too much pressure on them. This might happen by falling off a trampoline, bike, or skateboard. If we fall hard enough, our bones could bend, crack, or snap.

Different Kinds of Fractures

Fracture	Description
Complete	Bone is broken into two pieces.
Greenstick	Bone cracks on only one side.
Single	Bone breaks in one place.
Comminuted	Bone is crushed or breaks into two pieces or more.
Bending	Bone bends but doesn't break.
Open	Bone breaks through the skin.

First Aid for Bones

We should keep our bones healthy because we'll have the same ones for life. These tips can help your bones work well.

1. Eat foods that will help your bones grow and stay strong. These include foods with calcium and vitamin D, such as yogurt or milk.
2. Protect your bones by avoiding dangerous activities and wearing protective clothing, such as helmets, when playing sports.

10

I saw Devin's nose poking through the fence and rolled my eyes. He waved his cap back and forth to get my attention. "Great hit!" I ignored him and hoped he'd just go away. He didn't. "Hey Adam, what's up? Something wrong?"

The coach answered, "Might be a broken bone." My team gathered around me.

"Don't worry, Adam," Devin said. My dad is here, and he knows first aid. He'll know what to do." He turned toward the stands. "Dad! Come here!"

Devin and his dad rushed to my side. "Where does it hurt?" Mr. Smith asked. I touched a painful place several inches below my elbow. It was pink and seemed to be growing larger.

He gently examined my injured arm. "It's swelling already. You could have a broken bone in your arm," he said. "I think you should go to the hospital."

"I'll call your parents," my coach said.

"It's OK, I'll take him," Mr. Smith said. "That way we won't waste any time. Tell his parents to meet us at Children's Memorial." He looked around. "Before we go, I'll need ice and someone's shirt."

Devin paused for a minute, then took off his beloved Rockbirds shirt and gave it to his dad.

"Thanks, son. We need something to support Adam's arm before we move him." He tied the sleeves around my shoulders to make a sling and gently put my arm in it. He packed ice from the team's water cooler around my swelling arm.

"Now we're ready," he said. "Do you think you can stand up now?" I nodded, and he helped me to my feet.

"I'll come, too," Devin said. "To keep you company."

"Thanks," I said and really meant it. I didn't want to go to the hospital alone, and my teammates had to stay and finish the game. Both teams and all the fans clapped as I walked off the field.

Even though my parents met us at the hospital's emergency room, Devin still waited with me. He held a sports magazine open for us both to read.

When it was my turn to see a doctor, a nurse put me in a wheelchair and took me to have my arm X-rayed.

I placed my arm on a screen on a large electrical machine, and it took special pictures of the bones my arm. One of the bones was broken. To fix it, the doctor put a cast on my arm. He said it would help the bones heal properly.

On our way out of the hospital, Devin grabbed a pen. He wrote his name and number on my cast. "Give me a call if you feel like hanging out or if you need anything," he said.

"Thanks," I said, but doubted that I'd ever call him. Devin was nicer than I thought, but I couldn't imagine hanging out with him. What would we do? I'd be bored to death. I was sure my friends from the team would be all I'd need.

FYI
How an X-ray Machine Works

An X-ray machine is a lot like a camera. Instead of visible light, however, it uses X-rays to expose the film. When the X-rays hit the film, they expose it just as light would. Since bone, fat, muscle, tumors, and other masses all absorb X-rays at different levels, the image on the film lets you see distinct structures inside the body because of the different levels of exposure on the film.

Wilhelm Conrad Röntgen discovered the X-ray on November 8, 1895. The images produced by X-rays are due to the varying absorption rates of different tissues. Calcium in bones absorbs X-rays the most, so bones look white on a film recording of the X-ray image, called a radiograph. Fat and other soft tissues absorb less and look gray. Air absorbs the least, so lungs look black on a radiograph.

Besides, I knew that none of my friends would want to hang out with him.

Turns out, I was completely wrong about everything.

The cast was like a thick, clunky prison for my arm, and the doctor said I'd have to wear it for at least six weeks. I found out the first night

FYI

All About Casts

A cast is a hard shell-like bandage made out of white plaster or fiberglass. It holds a broken bone in place until it heals. Fiberglass casts can be different colors and have designs on them. Some are even waterproof so people can go swimming!

Each cast is made to specially fit the person who wears it. First, the doctor wraps soft cotton around the broken bone. Next, a thick layer of plaster or fiberglass circles around the cotton. The plaster and fiberglass harden to form a strong covering.

To keep a cast working properly, you should:

1. Keep the cast dry. Put plastic over it when bathing. Use a hair dryer to dry it off if it accidentally gets wet.
2. Keep sand, mud, and other dirt away from your cast.
3. Don't place any objects inside your cast.
4. Don't remove your cast. Only your doctor has the special tools needed to cut the cast off without injuring your skin.

that those six weeks were going to be some of the longest and most difficult of my life. The doctor told me and my parents to keep the arm elevated to help prevent swelling. My parents made me sit on the sofa and relax. They piled extra pillows on the armrest and told me to rest my cast there. It was uncomfortable, but they said my arm had to be high above my heart so that the extra liquid would flow toward my body, making the swelling go down.

Since my arm still really hurt, Dad gave me aspirin for the pain and put ice on the cast. I relaxed and moved my fingers slowly like the doctor had instructed, being careful not to let the melting ice leak on me. If the cast gets wet, it can get soggy and won't hold my bone in place as it should.

Things got a little better after the first night. There was less pain than the day before. Still, there were things the doctor didn't warn me about. The cast was clunky and made it hard to do even simple things, such as writing. With my arm trapped in fiberglass, I couldn't move my wrist. My writing looked like chicken scratches. Taking a bath took forever, too. First, I had to get ready by wrapping two layers of plastic bags around my cast, so it wouldn't get wet.

Then came the harder part—trying to hold on to slippery soap and wash myself with just one hand. Not being able to wash the skin under my cast wasn't fun either. It itched like crazy. I wanted to stick a ruler inside to scratch myself, but that wasn't allowed. The doctor said I could cut my arm or cause an infection.

The very worst thing about the cast was not playing baseball. When I felt better, I went to some of the practices. I couldn't throw, hit, or catch, and for the first time I understood what Devin must have felt like. All I could do was sit like a lump and watch—which was not fun. My friends were too busy practicing and working out to talk to me much, so I stopped going after a while.

One week after I broke my arm, I found Devin's neatly folded T-shirt on my bed. Mom had washed it for him. I walked to his house to return the shirt, and Devin invited me in to play games. Since I had nothing better to do, I said yes.

Devin's house was nothing like the geeky place I imagined. His room was a lot like mine. Baseball pennants and posters of his favorite players decorated the walls. Since the day was nice, after we were done playing board games,

we decided to go in the backyard and enjoy the sun. It didn't seem to matter to him that I had a cast and couldn't do much. We just relaxed and played on the swing that was outside on the lawn. I had so much fun that before I knew it, the sun was setting, and I had to go home for supper.

That was just the first of many fun summer afternoons in Devin's company. He introduced me to some of his other friends, and we watched movies, roasted hot dogs and marshmallows over bonfires, and held checker championships.

FYI

When a Bone Breaks

It can be scary when you break a bone. Knowing the right things to do can help you get better faster.

1. Don't move a bone you think might be broken. This could make it worse.
2. Keep the bone from moving by making a splint or sling.
3. Call 911 or have a professional health-care provider or family member take you to the hospital emergency room.
4. Keep the broken bone raised slightly above the level of your heart to decrease swelling.
5. Place ice over the broken bone to decrease swelling.

Thanks to Devin, I discovered that I enjoyed other things besides baseball, like camping, hiking in the woods, and fishing off the pier.

In July, my mom threw a big party for my birthday. I invited both my baseball teammates and Devin and my new friends. I worried for two weeks about the party. Would my team like the games I had planned? Or would they think the party was boring? Would everyone get along? I didn't want my teammates to make fun of Devin and my other new friends.

Luckily, I didn't have anything to worry about. My teammates liked movies, checkers, and the bonfire just as much as my new friends did. My teammates even seemed to like Devin, especially after he showed them some sneaky checker moves.

Six weeks after I broke my arm, the doctor removed my cast. My muscles were smaller and weaker, but I knew that with some work my arm would be back to normal, and I could play baseball again.

After that, games were never the same for me though. I always made sure to wave to my favorite fan Devin before batting. It turned out that he was our team's lucky charm after all.

Photo of Me
with My Cast

Signatures

Tell Your Story:
"When My Arm Broke"

rockbirds

How it happened:

When it happened:

Doctor's name:

Compare
your X-ray
to this one.

This is a
carpal bone.

This is a
metacarpal
bone.

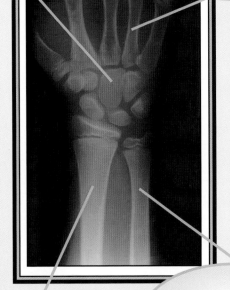

This is the
ulna bone.

This is the
radius bone.

Internet Sites

The Big Story on Bones
www.kidshealth.org/kid/body/bones_SW.html

Kids' Health: Broken Bones
**www.cyh.com/HealthTopics/HealthTopicDetails
  Kids.aspx?p=335&np=285&id=1569#6**

Science News for Kids: Bone Experiment
**www.sciencenewsforkids.org/articles/20030723/
  LZActivity.asp**

Your Gross and Cool Body: The Skeletal System
**yucky.kids.discovery.com/noflash/body/
  pg000124.html**

Books to Read

Hansen, Rosanna. *Bones!: All Kinds of Hands, All Kinds of Feet.* New York: Scholastic, 2002.

Parker, Steve. *Skeleton.* New York: DK Publishing, 2004.

Royston, Angela. *Broken Bones.* Chicago: Heinemann Library, 2004.

Weitzman, Elizabeth. *Let's Talk about Having a Broken Bone.* New York: PowerKids Press, 1997.

Ziefert, Harriet. *You Can't See Your Bones with Binoculars: a Guide to Your 206 Bones.* Maplewood, N.J.: Blue Apple Books, 2003.

Glossary

aspirin—a drug that relieves pain and reduces fever

baseball—a game played with a bat and ball and two teams of nine players each

bone—one of the hard, white parts that make up the skeleton of a person or an animal

bone marrow—the soft, jelly-like substance inside bones that is used to make blood cells

calcium—a soft, silver-white chemical compound found in certain foods as well as teeth and bones

cast—a hard plaster or fiberglass covering that supports a broken bone

cell—a basic, microscopic part of an animal or plant

elevated—to keep something lifted up

fiberglass—a strong insulating material made from fine threads of glass, used in casts

first aid—emergency care given to an injured or sick person before he or she is examined by a doctor

fracture—to break or crack something, especially a bone

mineral—a substance found in nature that is not an animal or a plant

muscle—one of the parts of your body that produces movement; your muscles are attached to your skeleton and pull on your bones to make them move

periosteum—the outer layer of a bone

protein—a substance found in all living plant and animal cells; foods, such as meat, cheese, eggs, beans, and fish, are sources of protein in your diet

sling—a loop of cloth used to support a broken arm

splint—a piece of wood, plastic, or metal used to support an injured or broken limb

swelling—growing larger, greater, or stronger

tumor—an abnormal lump or mass of tissue in the body

X-ray—an invisible high-energy beam of light that can pass through solid objects; X-rays are used to take pictures of teeth, bones, and organs inside the body.

Index

aspirin, 19

blood cells, 9

bones
    adult, 9
    broken, 9, 11, 13, 17, 23
    calcium in, 15
    cells in, 9
    first aid for, 10, 11
    fracture of, 10
    layers of, 9
    marrow, 9
    minerals in, 9
    proteins in, 9

cast, 13, 17, 19, 23, 25
    bathing with, 19, 21
    care of, 17
    fiberglass, 17, 19
    itching under, 21
    plaster, 17
    removal of, 17, 25
    water on, 17, 19
    writing with, 19
coach 5, 9

elbow, 11

fans 5, 7, 13, 25
fracture, 10

heart, 19, 23
home plate, 5, 7
hospital, 11, 13, 23

ice, 11, 13, 19, 23

nurse, 13

organs, 9

pain, 9, 19
periosteum, 9

radiograph, 15
Röntgen, Conrad, 15

skeleton, 9
sling, 13, 23
splint, 23
strike, 5, 7
swelling, 11, 13, 19, 23

team spirit, 5
tissue, 9, 15

umpire, 5, 7

wheelchair, 13

X-ray, 13, 15